ANCIENT CIVILIZATIONS

The Ancient Greeks

PAT TAYLOR

HEINEMANN
EDUCATIONAL

Acknowledgements

The author and publishers are grateful to the following for permission to reproduce copyright photographs: Photographers' Library, p. 7; Michael Holford, pp. 9, 15; H.L. Pierce Fund, Museum of Fine Arts, Boston, p.10; Sonia Halliday Photographs, pp. 22, 25; Ancient Art and Architecture Collection/Ronald Sheridan, pp. 24, 29.

Designed by Miller, Craig and Cocking.

Illustrated by Tony Maguire

Printed in Spain

by Mateu Cromo Artes Graficas SA

Heinemann Educational,
a division of Heinemann Educational Books Ltd,
Halley Court, Jordan Hill, Oxford OX2 8EJ

OXFORD LONDON EDINBURGH
MADRID ATHENS BOLOGNA PARIS
MELBOURNE SYDNEY AUCKLAND SINGAPORE TOKYO
IBADAN NAIROBI HARARE GABORONE
PORTSMOUTH NH (USA)

0 435 04207 6 softback
0 435 04360 9 hardback

Contents

Introduction

Greece is a rocky country and many of the people live near the sea. There are many islands.

MACEDONIA

THRACE

CHALKIDIKE

Mount Olympus

EPIRUS

THESSALY

Troy

AEGEAN SEA

EUBOEA

LESBOS

Ithaca

Delphi

SKYROS

BOEOTIA

CHIOS

Thebes

IONIA

ARCHAEA

Athens

Marathon

ELIS

Mycenae

Ephesus

Olympia

Argos

MESSENIA

DELOS

Sparta

NAXOS

LACONIA

KOS

MEDITERRANEAN SEA

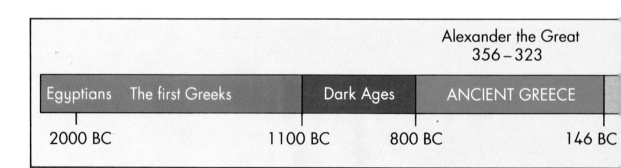

			Alexander the Great 356–323	
Egyptians	The first Greeks	Dark Ages	ANCIENT GREECE	
2000 BC	1100 BC	800 BC		146 BC

People lived in Greece from earliest times. Different groups of people organized their lives in different ways. They did not think of themselves as Greeks. By 800 BC, villages began to grow into towns. Some of the Greeks made city-states. They traded with each other and with other countries. Some of the city-states like Athens became very rich. Much of the evidence we have from Ancient Greece is from Athens. The people made beautiful vase paintings and statues. They wrote stories, poems and plays. They knew about science and maths. We still use many of their ideas. Some of the letters in our alphabet come from Greek letters.

Sometimes the city-states fought each other. Sometimes they fought together against other countries. In 499 BC they started to fight against Persia. Alexander the Great ruled all of Greece but when he died his land was split up.

The Romans took control of Greece in 146 BC.

You can see this marked on the timeline below.

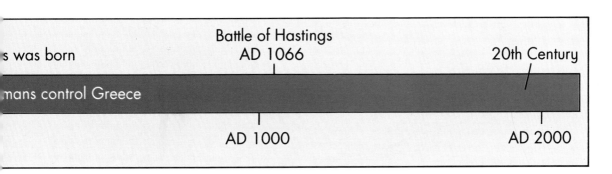

Gods and goddesses

The Greeks believed in many gods and goddesses. They controlled everything, from the weather to the way people felt. The Greeks thought that some of them lived on Mount Olympus. There are many stories about Greek gods and goddesses which we can read today.

These are some of the Greek gods and goddesses.

Hermes
Messenger of the gods.

Zeus
The most important god.

Hera
Wife of Zeus and queen of heaven.

Apollo
God of music. People went to his temple if they wanted to know about the future.

Athene
Goddess of wisdom.

The Greeks built temples in every town. Each temple was for a particular god or goddess. People went to the temple to pray. Sometimes they took a gift to please the god. If this was an animal the priest would sacrifice (kill) it.

One temple still standing today is the Parthenon. It is in Athens and was built for the goddess Athene.

This is the Parthenon. It had an enormous statue of Athene in it.

Clothes

Greek people wore loose clothes because Greece is a warm country. We can tell what they wore from their vase paintings and statues. Most people wore a tunic called a chiton. It was made from two rectangular pieces of cloth with holes for head and arms. Girls and boys dressed alike in short chitons. Men and women wore long ones. The Greeks also wore a cloak called a himation.

This is a Greek family with their slaves.

This is a Greek lady having a necklace put on her. It is from a vase painting.

Rich people's clothes were made of wool or linen. Sometimes they were brightly coloured. They wore boots or sandals. The women wore make-up, and on special occasions they might wear a fine wig.

Poor people and slaves did not wear shoes, and their clothes were usually made from wool.

Food

The Greeks ate a lot of fish. They only had big pieces of meat at festivals. They ate small birds like thrushes and swallows more often. They made sausages. They had lentils, radishes, celery and beans. They ate cheese, cakes and fruit, and used honey instead of sugar. The women, or their slaves, ground corn to make flour and bread. They made wine from grapes.

Many Greeks lived by the sea and caught fish to eat. We can see from this vase painting that they used a rod and line. They also used pots to catch lobsters.

Men and women did not eat meals together. The men lay on couches and were given the food by slaves. They had plates made from pottery. They ate with a metal spoon and knife or with their fingers. There was often music and dancing after the meal. Women and children usually ate together.

Some men at a dinner party.

Children

In most parts of Ancient Greece, boys were seen as more important than girls. Boys whose families could pay started school when they were six. They learned to read, do sums and write, and to enjoy poetry and music. They did not have desks, and they wrote on wax boards with a sharp pen. The girls helped their mothers in the house. They would cook, weave and do housework. Some girls were taught to read and write by their mothers. In Sparta, girls went to school and learned to be fit and strong.

This boy is being taught to write.

These Greek toys have been found. We know that when children died they were buried with their toys.

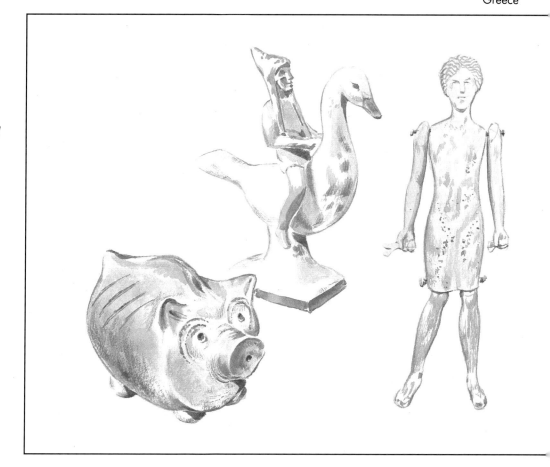

Greek children played with toys which were made of clay or leather.

When she was 15 a girl threw away her toys and married a man chosen by her father.

When he was 16 an Athenian boy trained for a job, perhaps as a craftsman. When he was 18 he became a citizen and could vote. Slaves and women were not allowed to vote.

13

Health and illness

The Ancient Greeks tried to keep fit and well. They thought that the gods made them ill. If they were ill they went to sleep near the temple of the god Asclepius. They thought that this would make them better. They also made medicine from plants.

This person is sleeping near the temple of Asclepius to try to get better.

These are the tools which Greek doctors used. The cup is to catch blood and the saw is to cut off legs and arms. The tweezers are to pull out spearheads and the spoon is for medicine.

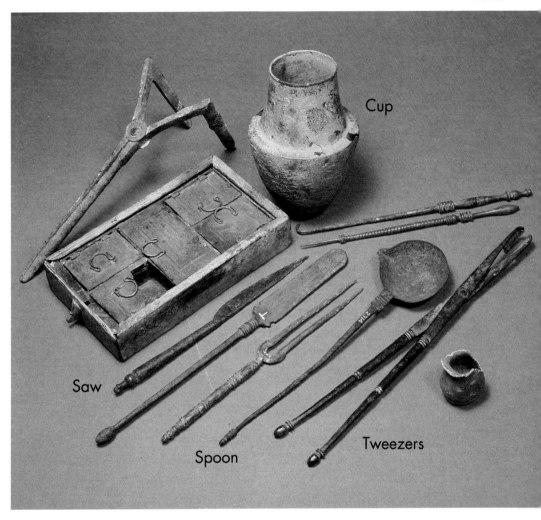

Cup

Saw

Spoon

Tweezers

Greek doctors had new ideas about why a person became ill. The most famous of these doctors was called Hippocrates. He did not think that illness came from the gods. His ideas about how a doctor should work still affect us today.

Buildings

Some Greek buildings still stand today. These are the buildings that everybody used and saw as important. They were built by stonemasons and carpenters and their slaves. Some of them took many years to finish. They had columns to hold the roofs up. There are three types: Doric, Ionic and Corinthian. Stones were carried on wagons from the quarries. They were lifted by ropes and pulleys and held together with small pieces of wood and metal.

Houses were made of mud bricks. They were not built to last. Poor people's houses were very simple. Rich people had more rooms. Their houses were built around a courtyard. There were large, cool rooms but not much furniture. Men and women had their own rooms.

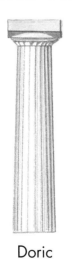

Doric

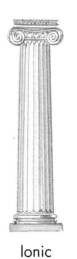

Ionic

Corinthian

The columns which the Greeks built were plain at first, but later they decorated them more.

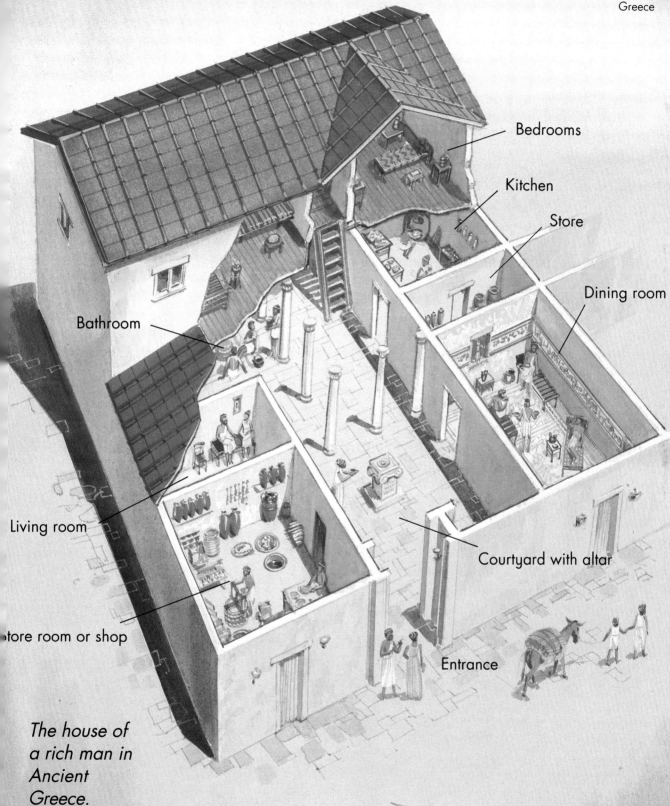

Bedrooms

Kitchen

Store

Dining room

Bathroom

Living room

tore room or shop

Courtyard with altar

Entrance

*The house of
a rich man in
Ancient
Greece.*

Town life

Ancient Greece was divided into small areas called city-states. Only Athens and Sparta were big. Each city-state had its own laws. Sometimes it had its own coins and army. At its centre was a town with a fortified hill called an acropolis.

Athens was a democracy. This means that every man born in Athens, unless he was a slave, could vote on how things were run.

Not guilty

Guilty

These discs were used in the law courts. They say if a person was guilty or not guilty.

In the middle of the town was the agora. The main buildings were here and it was a meeting place. There were bankers' stalls, market stalls and law courts. People would walk round and chat. There were slaves for sale, boys being taught, and acrobats and musicians. Around the agora were the town houses. Craftsmen lived here. The fronts of their houses were their workshops.

The agora
was a very
busy place in
a Greek
town.

19

Trade and ships

The Ancient Greeks traded with other countries such as Egypt, Syria and Sicily. The Greeks found it easier to travel by sea than over land because of the mountains and poor roads. The Greeks could find where they were going by the stars. They built merchant ships to carry their goods. The ships carried slaves, wood, corn, iron and copper.

At first the Greeks bartered (swapped) their goods. Later, some city-states had their own coins. This is the 'owl' of Athens.

Leather ropes

Linen sail

Hull

Bow

Ram

Painted eye to keep evil spirits away or for the ship to see wh it was going

The merchant ships were made of wood and had a large hold to store the cargo. They had a sail and oars. They were slow and heavy but there were other Greek ships which were lighter. These were warships called triremes. In peacetime they could protect the merchant ships from pirates. They had a ram to hit other ships. They had three rows of oarsmen and could carry 200 men.

This is a trireme.

Stern

Steering oar

21

Country life

Most Greek people lived in the country and were farmers. It was a hard life. The soil was rocky and did not grow very good crops. It rained too much in the winter and too little in the summer. The summer was also very hot. Grapes grew on the sides of the hills. Olives grew on trees on the poor soil, just as they do today. Their oil was used for cooking and for making lamps. On the better soil the Greeks grew corn. They used oxen to plough. They kept donkeys, sheep and goats.

This is what Greece looks like now. It has not changed much since the time of the Ancient Greeks. It is a hot, dry and rocky place.

Here are some people at work in the country. You can see that the women and children had to work.

The roads were very poor and most people walked. Some people had horses and carts and rich people rode on horseback. As well as farmers there were carpenters to make and mend carts. There were herdsmen to look after the animals. There were also miners who dug for silver.

The Olympic Games

The Greeks liked sport. Every day they did some exercises. We think that the Olympic Games began in 776 BC. They were held in Olympia every four years. The games were part of Greek religious life. They started with a sacrifice to Zeus. Some events, like chariot racing, are not in the Olympic Games today. Other events, like the pentathlon, are. To win the pentathlon, athletes had to complete five events. These were discus throwing, javelin throwing, wrestling, running and long jumping. Winners of all races were given olive wreaths to wear on their heads.

This is a famous statue of a discus thrower. A Greek discus was a flat metal plate.

This is a Greek stadium. The athletes ran one or two stades. A stade was about 200 metres. The spectators sat on the stone seats.

Olympia had a stadium, baths and temples. We can still see the remains of some of these buildings.

The Olympic Games were stopped by the emperor Theodosius in AD 393. Then, in 1896, they were started again. They are still held every four years but there are no sacrifices. The games begin when an athlete lights a special flame with fire brought from Olympia.

25

Art and theatre

The Ancient Greeks enjoyed all kinds of art. As well as paintings, they liked music, poems and statues. Their vase paintings and statues tell us what they did and what they looked like. The statues took a long time to make and were usually painted. We do not know what their music sounded like but we know from vase paintings that they played harps and pipes.

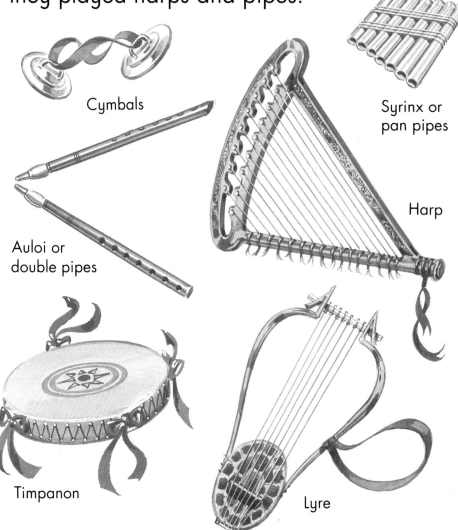

Cymbals

Syrinx or pan pipes

Auloi or double pipes

Harp

Timpanon

Lyre

We know that the Greeks had all these instruments because we can see them in vase paintings.

*Greek plays are still performed today.
This one is in an Ancient Greek theatre.*

Many Greek towns had an open-air theatre. They were only used for festivals. People watched about four plays, one after the other. The plays were either funny (comedies) or sad (tragedies). All the actors were men. They had to play more than one part. They wore masks to show who they were playing.

Great thinkers

The Greeks wanted to know about their world. Was it flat? What happened to the sun at night? Where were the stars in the day time? They would sit in the agora and talk, telling each other of their ideas. They wanted to know about water. Archimedes discovered why it overflowed and how to move it uphill.

This is the screw that Archimedes invented to take water uphill.

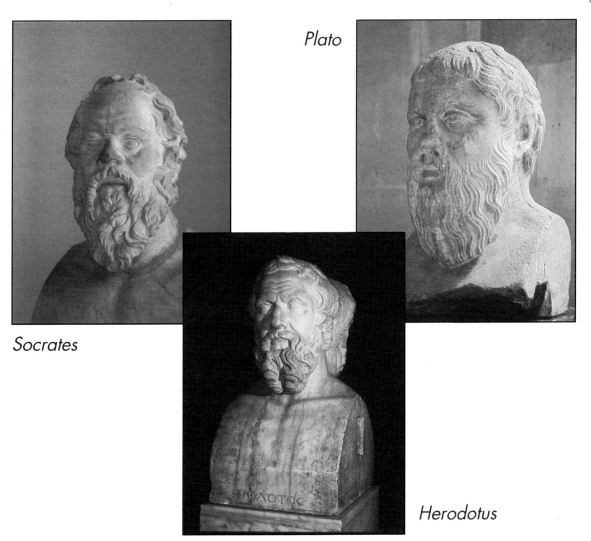

Plato

Socrates

Herodotus

These are statues of famous Greeks.

Some Greeks, like Pythagoras, studied maths and looked at shapes and angles. Some, like Socrates, wondered what made people behave the way they did, and thought about good and evil. Some, like Plato, thought about how countries should be ruled. Herodotus studied history, and we can learn a lot about the Greeks from his writing.

29

Famous stories

We know lots of stories about Greek people. Some of the stories were made up around things that really happened. There really was a war between Greece and Troy. The stories that are told about it in a book called The Iliad may not be true, but they are famous.

This shows the capture of Troy by the Greeks. The story is told in The Iliad.

We know much more about Alexander the Great. He was taught by an important thinker called Aristotle. He ruled Greece after his father Philip died. He won many battles and took over many lands. He ruled Egypt in the end and built a large city called Alexandria. After he died, all his land was split up and was later taken by the Romans.

This is a picture of Alexander the Great which was made out of small pieces of coloured tiles. It is called a mosaic.

31

Index